She taught me to eat artichokes

The Discovery of the Heart of Friendship

She Taught Me to Eat Artichokes

is dedicated

to the memory of Karen. Her friendship was worth waiting for. — MKS

to Anita — PM

© 1993 by Sta-Kris, Inc.

Illustrations copyright © 1993 by Paul Micich

Published by Sta-Kris, Inc., P.O. Box 1131, Marshalltown, Iowa 50158

Printed and bound in the Republic of Korea

Printed by Dong-A Publishing and Printing Co., Ltd.

ISBN 1-882835-11-5

The illustrations in this book were rendered in alkyd and pastels on linen.

The text was set in Linotype Hiroshige medium and bold.

Calligraphy by Sally Cooper Smith

Designed by Sally Cooper Smith and Paul Micich

store, or

, how you were supposed to prepare
"accident.

beside
was there to eat anyway.
strong

leaves that really are more like this

ichokes (and eggplants) really did have

or whatever it's called, pricked
a black velvet dress instead of a doll.
ack velvet dress. But when there wasn't a
osed to get one home to eat if I
, that was the first year there wasn't a

always bought lettuce and tomatoes

expect it, a common thread —
, you know
friendship.

is obviously not something you can tell

Sometimes we must wait

patiently for the treasures of life.

Sometimes those treasures wait

patiently for us.

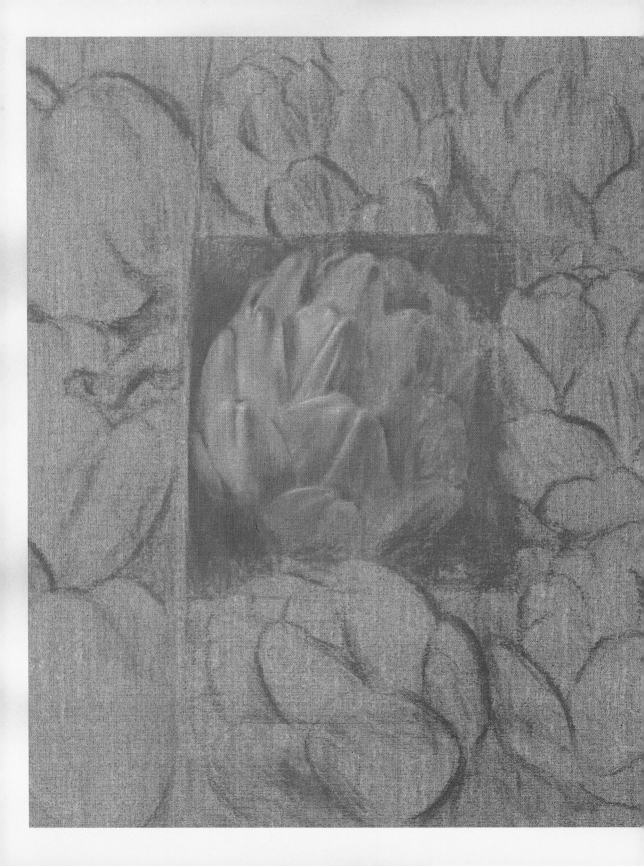

I'd seen artichokes in the produce aisle
before. *Of course, I can't remember the first
time I actually paid attention to them.* I did
know that they were always bunched one atop
the other, balancing like vegetables do along
the bin's edge.

But it was my habit to walk right on past, pretending not to
notice.

To be honest about it, I didn't know what artichokes were, how you were supposed to prepare them, or how you were supposed to eat them. *And what was there to eat, anyway?*

All I knew for sure was that they have those pointy leaves that really are more like thistles. I touched one once, after finally acknowledging that artichokes (and eggplants) really did have a place in the produce aisle. The leaf, or the petal, or whatever it's called, pricked my finger.

So then I wondered, how am I supposed to get one home to eat if I can't even pick it up to put in the cart? Besides, I always bought lettuce and tomatoes and green beans. They don't take much kitchen time, you know.

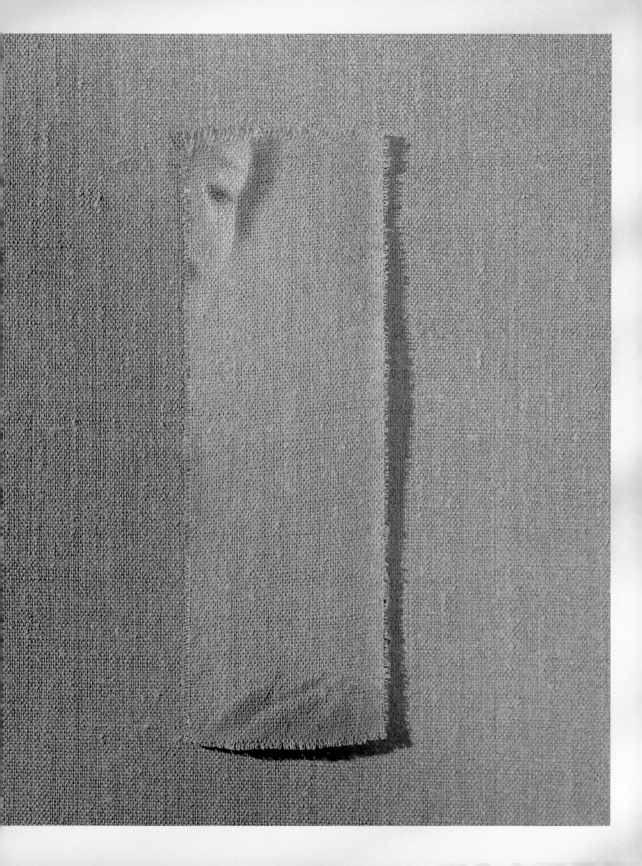

My neighbor knew how to fix artichokes,
although that's obviously not something you can tell
about a person right off.

The fact of the matter is, you couldn't tell much of
anything about her. That's how it is with people
sometimes. They nod. They say hello. They laugh —
politely. And most keep a cautious distance.

So you share a little conversation. Small talk.

"Hello!" I call to her from amidst my backyard
flower garden. **"We sure could use a good rain. This**
soil is hard as a rock."

"Don't worry," she calls back, over her shoulder.
"It'll rain Saturday, right after I wash my car."

We both chuckle at the notion. But then, she turns to go into her house. And I
get on with my digging and weeding. I must finish it so I can run to the store — to
buy lettuce and tomatoes and green beans. *Ignore the artichokes. They're too*
prickly. And anyway, they'd probably take too long to fix

— even if I knew how to fix them.

There were a few weeks that one summer when I didn't

go to the store, or even see the neighbor very much.

Our son was in a car accident. Suddenly, familiar routines

evaporated into endless days beside his hospital bed. Days

spent waiting for his body to get strong enough so doctors

could repair his knee.

The morning of surgery, she was there. The neighbor. "I thought you might want someone to sit with you for awhile," she said simply.

That's how it is with people sometimes. They're quiet. Thoughtful. And just when you've decided that life's hectic pace requires them to keep their distance, they have a way of surprising you.

But today, life's not hectic. Today, there is time. So you sit next to each other. And share a little more small talk.

"I just hate hospitals. They smell so antiseptic," I tell her.

"I know," she says. "They all look the same, no matter what color the walls are painted."

And as the hours wear on, we find ourselves treading closer to personal thoughts, inching toward intimate feelings.

"I'm scared for him," I offer in cautious invitation.

"I know," she replies. "That's why I thought you might want some extra company. I've been scared before, too."

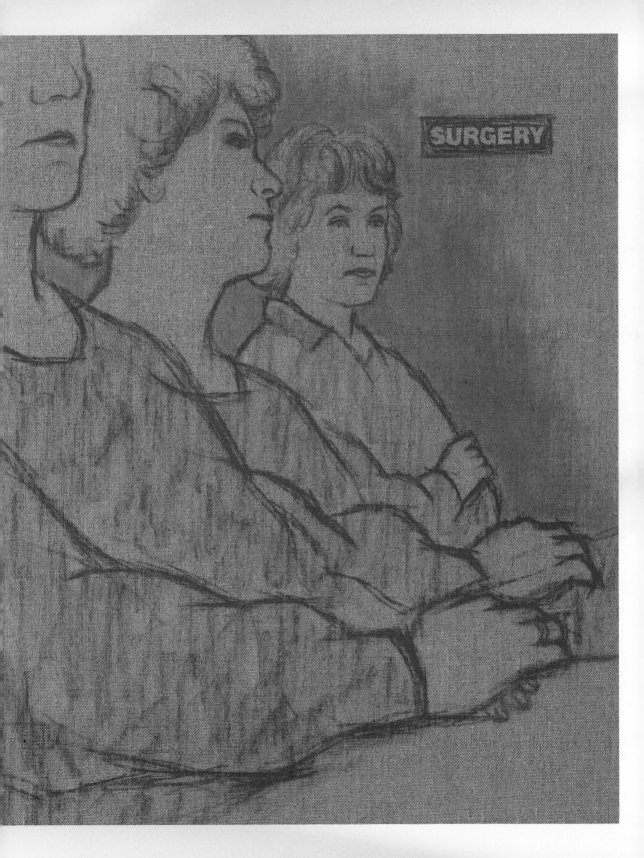

Groceries

Green beans
Tomatoes
Lettuce
Cereal
Milk
Bread
Macaroni
Juice

Weeks later, we bring our son home from the
hospital. And as his healing continues, it's back to
scurrying through the store, grabbing some lettuce
and tomatoes and green beans. A person can whip
up a good meal in no time with that produce.

I pause just long enough to watch someone looking over the artichokes. Carefully
studying the pile, finally selecting a couple. And I wonder if *she* pricks her fingers
as she lays the artichokes atop the other groceries in her cart.

There was our annual July Fourth barbecue. A traditional ending to a

traditional day. An aroma drifted across the patio, tantalizing guests who were too

hot for one more game of backyard volleyball, even though a steaming sun finally

had bowed to dusk's cool breezes.

She came. The neighbor. She smiled. She chatted. She even told a couple of
jokes
— *they were funny, no kidding!* It was her first time to join us, and she stayed the
evening.

That's how it is with people sometimes. Ones you assume only listen politely —
ones you assume only chuckle appropriately — slowly allow you to move inside
their borders.

So it is that this neighbor — who, like you, always seemed in a hurry — begins to
mold into a person whom you'd like to know better.

I go home happy, *feeling as though I've snatched an evening away from Time,*
trading in busy hours for a pleasant discovery.

The next day, of course, I'm back in that familiar routine. Dash to the store. Grab some lettuce and tomatoes and green beans. Everybody's in a rush for dinner tonight.

But I stop long enough to gingerly pick up an artichoke, wondering how to fix it.

And then, I put the artichoke back.

The holidays swept in on howling North winds,

whipping snow in reckless patterns until white covered

the last traces of autumn. Afterward, the moon appeared,

casting its mellow glow across the clean, silent land.

It was that cherished time of year, when the peace of
evening calls you outdoors to go caroling.

Curiously, I invited the neighbor first. We'd never sung together before, you
understand. *Now that I think about it, I didn't even know if she liked to sing!*

But she came. And she sang.

Our sounds of the season mingled with the falling snow to
fill up the soft night air. Later, we all settled around the
fireplace. The room was warm and fragrant with the scent
of pine. We sipped cider from steaming mugs, and we
shared stories about our own Christmases past.

"I remember the year I got a black velvet dress," I began, "instead of a doll. I knew I'd feel so grown-up in a black velvet dress. But when there wasn't a doll under the tree...I mean, that was the first year there wasn't a doll..."

The neighbor smiled. "I remember when my sister told me who Santa Claus really was. Or wasn't. I cried myself to sleep that Christmas Eve, because I thought the next morning would be like every other morning. I was so afraid the magic would be gone."

The shared memories brought smiles, laughter, a few tears and, at last, a sense of contentment. For slowly, from our treasured memories a kindred bond began to emerge.

That's how it is with people sometimes. When you least expect it, a common thread — golden, at that — begins to weave together the fabric of friendship.

After the holidays, it's back to more sensible meals. Stir up a casserole. Slap together some hamburgers. Quickly fill the cart with lettuce and tomatoes and green beans. *Oh, and one eggplant. I saw a recipe I would like to try. Even though it might take awhile.*

When her daughter graduated that spring, we celebrated the occasion on the

neighbor's back porch. Cold cuts and spicy baked beans. Slurpy watermelon and

lemonade so tart it made you pucker.

"Sometime," she shared, "I am going to have a dinner party. A nice one, with good china and crystal. We'll dress up."

The night of her party, I scurried to prepare dinner for the children. BLT's and chips — and green beans. *(Up with the noses, I know. But mothers are supposed to fix things that are good for you.)*

As I fussed in my own kitchen, I knew she'd be fussing in hers. I wondered what she would serve us.

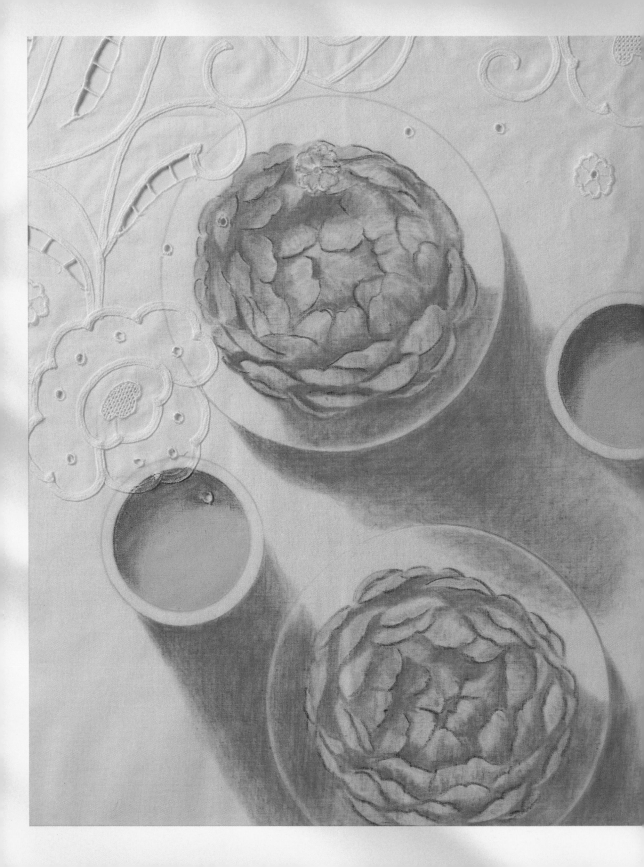

She served us artichokes! Each one in its own dish. Each one accompanied by a smaller dish of *(real)* melted butter.

"Take the petals off, one at a time," she explained as she pulled one gently from the flower's crown. "Dip the petal in the butter. Now, hold on to the tip and put the petal part way in your mouth."

She stopped and looked around the table.

"The warmth of the stewing has softened the petals, so they won't prick your fingers," she explained.

(How did she know?)

"Now, let your front teeth scrape off the meat as you pull the petal back out."

"Like this."

We peeled. We dipped. We scraped.

Slowly.

To savor.

We laughed. We joked. We shared. Never worrying about the hour of the evening.

We dripped butter on her Irish linen tablecloth. We enjoyed background music — *Mozart, I believe*. Artichoke petals, properly scraped of their meat, mounded in a bowl at the table's center. Surprisingly, the closer we got to the base of the crown, the more delicious and plentiful was the meat.

Finally, she leaned forward, to get our attention.

"You may think you've had the best the plant has to offer," she said. **"But actually, the best is yet to come. When you've peeled off all of your petals, you'll find a treat. A surprise. It's the heart of the artichoke. The gift of the plant."**

That's how it is with people sometimes. You peel the layers off one by one. Slowly. Patiently.

Making time.

Taking time.

Rewarded in small ways. And all the while, you're working toward a goal you didn't know was there.

As the stewing makes tender the artichoke petals, so too, do time and effort turn acquaintanceships into the tender treasure that is friendship.

That evening, in the glow of candlelight, and in the warmth which can only be felt among friends, each of us reached the heart of the artichoke.

We are most comfortable with the things we know the best.

But if we always avoid the unfamiliar,

how will we ever know what riches may be waiting for us,

deep within the heart?

A first encounter with an artichoke can be a perplexing and somewhat formidable experience, for the artichoke gives little clue from its appearance of the delights that wait within. The heart of the artichoke is surrounded — protected if you will — by both leaves and the choke or thistle. When properly prepared, the choke is easily removed and the small amount of meat on softened leaves yields a promise of what's to come.

To prepare artichokes, wash them in water, then cut off the stems at the base. Remove the small bottom leaves and any that are discolored. Cut about one inch off the top. You may trim off the thorny tips of each leaf with a scissors. (Do not use cast-iron or aluminum cooking utensils or non-stainless steel knives as they will turn the artichokes black.)

You can either cook or steam the artichokes.

To cook, place the artichokes in a large pot. Add enough water to cover the artichokes half-way. To prevent the artichokes from darkening, add one tablespoon vinegar or lemon juice per quart of water. Cover the pot and cook the artichokes for 20 to 45 minutes, depending upon size. Artichokes are done when a knife or fork can be inserted easily into the base and the outside leaves pull off handily.

To steam, place the artichokes upright on a steamer rack (available in many kitchenware stores) in a steamer kettle. Add water up to the base of the artichokes. Cover the pot and steam for 30 to 65 minutes, depending upon size. Artichokes are done when a knife or fork can be inserted easily into the base and the outside leaves pull off handily.

To serve the artichokes, place each artichoke on an individual plate or artichoke platter. While there are many sauces in which you can dip the meaty leaves and heart, the most common is melted butter with a squeeze of fresh lemon.

Mary Kay Shanley thought that she didn't like artichokes. But that was before she actually tasted an artichoke one very special evening. The author, her husband and two dogs (who eat anything!) live in West Des Moines, Iowa. They have two children in college and a third who is a college graduate. (Whew!)

Ms. Shanley has been writing for newspapers and magazines for almost 30 years. But she says no assignment — including meeting Presidents — can compare with the joy that has come from sharing this story about friendship.

Paul Micich, the illustrator of this story, eats artichokes, too. He also wins awards, including Gold and Silver awards from the Society of Illustrators of Los Angeles. His work has been included in shows and annuals for the Society of Illustrators of New York and the Communication Arts Illustration Annual.

But for all of that success, a career high point came in 1991 when his son, Ari Micich, served as the model for his father, who was commissioned to create illustrations for the new edition of that warm and wonderful story, "The Littlest Angel" written by Charles Tazewell. The Micich family lives in Des Moines, Iowa.

...ee days that summer when I didn't go...
...honest about it. I didn't know what artichok...
...see the neighbor very much. Our son was in...
...ly familiar routines evaporated into endl...
...how you were supposed to eat them. And...
...ospital bed. Days spent waiting for his bod...
...so doctors could repair his knee.

...knew for sure was that they have those...

...bed one once, after finally acknowledging th...

...in the produce aisle. The leaf, or the...
I remember the year...

...nger. — So then I wondered, how am I...
I'd feel so grown up
under the tree...

...even pick it up to put in the cart? Besid...

...how it is with people sometimes. When you...
...een beans. They don't take much kit...
...at that — begins to weave together the fabr...

...ighbor knew how to cut artichokes, although...